THE CALL OF THE RUNNING TIDE

THE CALL OF THE RUNNING TIDE

A Portrait of an Island Family

Nancy Price Graff

Photographs

Richard Howard

Little, Brown and Company
Boston   Toronto   London

Also by Nancy Price Graff and Richard Howard:

The Strength of the Hills: A Portrait of a Family Farm

Text copyright © 1992 by Nancy Price Graff
Photographs copyright © 1992 by Richard Howard

First Edition

Library of Congress Cataloging-in-Publication Data

Graff, Nancy Price, 1953–
    The call of the running tide : a portrait of an island family / by
    Nancy Price Graff ; photographs by Richard Howard. — 1st ed.
        p.   cm.
    Summary: Captures the way of life of the Joyces, a fishing family
    on Swans Island off the coast of Maine, as they spend their lives
    harvesting the bounty of the sea.
    ISBN 0-316-32278-4
    1. Swans Island (Me. : Island) — Social life and customs — Juvenile
    literature.   2. Fishing — Maine — Swans Island (Island) — Juvenile
    literature.   3. Joyce family — Juvenile literature.   4. Swans Island
    (Me. : Island) — Social life and customs — Pictorial works — Juvenile
    literature.   5. Fishing — Maine — Swans Island (Island) — Pictorial
    works — Juvenile literature.   6. Joyce Family — Pictorial works —
    Juvenile literature.   [1. Swans Island (Me. : Island) — Social life
    and customs.   2. Fishing — Maine — Swans Island (Island)   3. Joyce
    family.]   I. Howard, Richard (Richard Huntington) ,ill.   II. Title.
    F27.H3G73   1992
    974.1'45 — dc20   91-11341

10 9 8 7 6 5 4 3 2 1

WOR

Published simultaneously in Canada
by Little, Brown & Company (Canada) Limited

Printed in the United States of America

To my parents
    N. P. G.

To my wife, Brett, and to Miles
                R. H.

THE CALL OF THE
RUNNING TIDE

A Portrait of an Island Family

Nancy Price Graff

Photographs
Richard Howard

Little, Brown and Company
Boston   Toronto   London

Also by Nancy Price Graff and Richard Howard:
The Strength of the Hills: A Portrait of a Family Farm

J
974.1
Gra

Library of Congress Cataloging-in-Publication Data

Graff, Nancy Price, 1953–
    The call of the running tide : a portrait of an island family / by
Nancy Price Graff ; photographs by Richard Howard. — 1st ed.
        p.   cm.
    Summary: Captures the way of life of the Joyces, a fishing family
on Swans Island off the coast of Maine, as they spend their lives
harvesting the bounty of the sea.
    ISBN 0-316-32278-4
    1. Swans Island (Me. : Island) — Social life and customs — Juvenile
literature.   2. Fishing — Maine — Swans Island (Island) — Juvenile
literature.   3. Joyce family — Juvenile literature.   4. Swans Island
(Me. : Island) — Social life and customs — Pictorial works — Juvenile
literature.   5. Fishing — Maine — Swans Island (Island) — Pictorial
works — Juvenile literature.   6. Joyce Family — Pictorial works —
Juvenile literature.   [1. Swans Island (Me. : Island) — Social life
and customs.   2. Fishing — Maine — Swans Island (Island)   3. Joyce
family.]   I. Howard, Richard (Richard Huntington) ,ill.   II. Title.
    F27.H3G73   1992
    974.1'45 — dc20   91-11341

10 9 8 7 6 5 4 3 2 1

WOR

Published simultaneously in Canada
by Little, Brown & Company (Canada) Limited

Printed in the United States of America

The Gulf of Maine is a vast and restless place. Even on sweltering summer days, when not a breath of air moves inland, the wind blows here. Waves swell and crest in an endless rhythm that stretches back before the time of man. Clouds billow and sail across the sky or hover in long, thin wisps on the western horizon above the inland mountains. Every day the sun burns a path across a sky that is breathtakingly big and bright and blue.

8

Change is a way of life here. Neither the sky nor the water stays the same from minute to minute. The light changes, the winds shift, the tides themselves are always coming or going, rising or ebbing, arriving or leaving.

Life in such an unstable environment seems out of place and vulnerable, but it thrives here. Seagulls wheel and somersault in the clear air. Terns fly in close formation, skimming over the surface of the water in undulating swells that follow the dark contours of the waves. Dolphins frolic, their glistening bodies arcing out of the water with graceful precision. The water itself is one of the most fertile fishing grounds in the world, and the ocean floor teems with the movement of crabs and lobsters, sea urchins and cucumbers, starfish and scallops.

Even humans have made a home for themselves here, although they are few in number and widely scattered. Of the more than three thousand islands off the coast of Maine, fewer than one hundred are inhabited. Some of the islands are large, like Mount Desert, and connected to the mainland by bridges that act as arteries to connect the islands' residents to the pulse of

mainland life. Some of the islands are remote, like Matinicus, which lies more than a two-hour journey out to sea by a ferry that makes the trip just once a month — if weather permits.

Swans Island lies five miles offshore and more than two-thirds of the way up the coast of Maine. It is a rocky, butterfly-shaped island no more than twelve miles across from wing tip to wing tip. Cradled within the crescent of its wings is one of the finest harbors on the Atlantic seaboard.

When the weather is fair and the machinery is behaving, the ferry makes the forty-five-minute crossing to Swans Island six times a day in summer and four times a day in winter. During July and August, the ferry is full nearly every crossing. It rides low in the water under the weight of cars and tourists and any number of the island's six hundred summer residents, many of whom lounge against the rails to watch the neighboring islands slip past. Off season, which means the other ten months of the year, a smaller ferry satisfies the needs of Swans Island's three hundred fifty full-time residents.

But not everyone has come by ferry to this stony speck of land. The Joyces arrived one hundred eighty-five years ago, before the days of ferries, back when people depended on sloops and schooners and other boats with sails as white and big as clouds to carry them where they needed to go and to keep them in touch with people beyond the rim of their horizons. Almost every day since then, Joyces have gone down to the sea in their boats. They have fished for mackerel and cod and lobster by sail and oar and diesel engine. They have clung to this small island through surging storms and long, dark winters with the same stubborn strength that binds a mussel to a rock.

This is the story of a year on Swans Island, where Spencer and Wendy Joyce live with their children, Joshua, Jaime, and Emmie, and of the way of life they have made for themselves surrounded by the bountiful and fickle sea.

At night the lobster boats of the Swans Island fleet bob at their moorings inside Burnt Coat Harbor and ride the waves and tides like a flock of sleeping gulls. In midsummer, however, the boats get little rest. A day of lobstering begins in the dim light before dawn when the lobsters are hungry, the breezes are often soft, and the sea is generally calm. Later in the day the winds and waves will kick up as the afternoon heat builds. The changeable conditions then will make the hard work of lobstering even harder, so lobstermen have adjusted the hours of their workday to the ways of the sea and begin their work early.

13

Spencer Joyce arrives at the wharf this morning around four o'clock. Just a few hours ago thunderstorms swirled around the island and filled the night sky with ragged light, but they have moved out toward the open water, and a thick morning fog has rolled in. If it were not for the fog, fourteen-year-old Joshua would have risen with his father this morning, as he has nearly every morning this summer to lobster with his grandfather. Llewellyn Joyce, Josh's grandfather and Spencer's father, would also be here if the dawn were fair and pink. Llewellyn has spent close to three-quarters of a century on the water, and by now his early morning habits are as regular as the tides. But as Llewellyn has grown older, he has stopped taking the added risks of navigating a boat and hauling lobster traps in thick fog. He and Josh will head out in an hour or two when the warmth of the rising sun begins to scatter the fog.

The wharf is the heart of this island, and lobstering is its heartbeat. From long before dawn to long after dark, lobstermen and their families mill about, pickup trucks arrive and leave, and boat engines hiccup and throb. Here there is always news, the familiar rhythms of daily work, and the strong smell of old fish and new sweat.

Spencer grew up in a house overlooking this wharf, and he no longer notices its smells or the pulse of the tides against its pilings. This morning, after pausing to share coffee and news with some of the other lobstermen,

Spencer takes his small skiff out to where his lobster boat is moored. Slowly he is swallowed by the yawning grayness, but he is not worried about getting lost. His family has fished this harbor for at least eight generations. He doesn't need his eyes to see its scalloped coves and rocky shores.

In a few minutes the engine of Spencer's boat, *The Daily Bread,* rumbles to life, coughing and sputtering like an old man clearing his throat. When the rumbling settles to a low throb, Spencer brings his thirty-five-foot lobster boat back to the wharf where his sternman, Bobby Treadwell, is waiting. Both men are dressed in the uniform of their trade: yellow waterproof bib pants, heavy rubber black boots, and layers of T-shirts and old sleeveless sweatshirts that can be peeled off as the day warms. Bobby jumps aboard and helps ready the boat for the day's work.

Most of the preparations were completed the evening before. The boat

was washed and scrubbed. The fuel tank was filled. Two barrels of salted herring, lobsters' favorite summer food, were purchased at the wharf and lowered carefully to the boat's deck. The herring has ripened overnight. In the still morning air, its sharp smell mingles with diesel exhaust and the pungent aroma of sea salt.

By four-thirty, Bobby has cast off the dock lines, and Spencer is navigating through the fog and pale light, around the moored lobster boats and toward the mouth of the harbor. Within five minutes, nothing is visible but the dense fog and the flat, calm water dead ahead. Even the pulsing light of Hockamock

Head lighthouse at the entrance to the harbor is barely and only briefly visible as the boat slips out into the open sea.

Despite conditions such as these, early morning is Spencer's favorite time of day. Like all lobstermen, he lives with the unpredictability of nature. From day to day he does not know if the weather will be fair, if a storm will carry off his traps, or if the lobsters will choose his bait over someone else's. Nevertheless, the excitement of the day's promise lures him like bait in the early morning to the four hundred traps that lie before him waiting to be hauled.

Eleven minutes out, Spencer spots the fluorescent orange and black paint of his first lobster buoy bobbing on the waves. He positions the boat at the farthest reach of the buoy's rope and cuts the engine. Keeping one hand on the wheel to guide the boat, Spencer picks up his gaff and reaches into the water with it to hook the floating buoy. Behind him, Bobby has filled two empty bait  bags with herring and hung them by their hooks from the rim of the bait barrels. Now he stands at the rail, waiting. The hard work is about to begin.

The ease and speed with which Spencer and Bobby work disguises the complexity of what they are doing. Using the gaff, Spencer pulls the buoy up on the rail of the boat and scoots it down beside the wheelhouse, or cabin. With his other hand he threads the buoy's warp, or rope, into a hydraulic hauler, which quickly hauls the trap the forty feet up from the ocean floor. Midway along the warp, the toggle surfaces. This small buoy keeps the long lobster lines from lying on the bottom and snarling with rocks when the tide is low. Spencer grabs the toggle and tosses it alongside the larger lobster buoy. Meanwhile, the lobstering warp coils rapidly into a nest at Spencer's feet, slopping him and Bobby with seaweed and slime. As the first trap emerges from the deep, Bobby grabs it and pulls it onto the boat's rail. In a

few moments a second trap also emerges from the green water, and Spencer hauls it, too, onto the rail.

A lobster trap has no moving parts except the lobsters it catches. Its design has changed little in one hundred years, although wire is now more commonly used than wood for the trap's frame because it sits better on the ocean bottom and is more durable. Lobsters are lured into the fishing head of the trap by the rotting bait suspended in its bag inside the trap. Once inside, the lobsters fall to the floor of the trap's first parlor and quickly discover that the netting guyed, or strung, within the trap has caught them in its web. They can struggle farther into the trap, looking for a way to escape, but all their labors will only bring them into a deeper parlor.

The ocean supports more than two hundred thousand species of marine life, and lobster is not the only one that finds salted herring bait appealing. The traps seem alive with thrashing lobsters, dozens of snapping rock crabs and quick crabs, flopping fish, spiky sea urchins, wriggling sea fleas, and scuttling hermit crabs. All of them have been enticed by the meal the

lobstermen have offered and now find themselves trapped. None of them is happy, and their protective instincts tell them to fight. Every claw in the trap is raised and cocked, angry and ready to do battle.

Spencer and Bobby slip off the bungee cords that keep the trap lids closed and begin to sort through their catch. They work quickly, avoiding the claws as best they can. The claws of lobsters that are clearly of legal size are banded with thick rubber bands, and the lobsters are tossed into water-filled barrels behind the wheelhouse. The bands are not for the protection of the lobstermen, who will have little occasion to handle the lobsters again, but to prevent the lobsters from damaging or even killing each other before they are sold. Lobsters that need to be measured are tossed still thrashing above the wheel onto the bulkhead. Spencer will get to them in a minute. Lobsters that are obviously undersize are tossed back into the sea, spinning through the air like so many shooting stars.

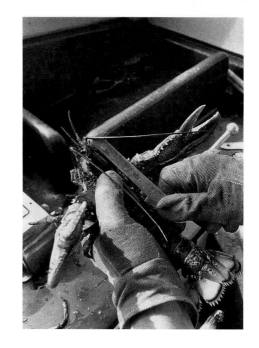

When the lobsters have been sorted, Spencer or Bobby turns each trap upside down and shakes it over the side of the boat. Crabs, urchins, fish, starfish, sea cucumbers, eels, and small stingrays all rain down. Then Bobby takes the scraps of old lobster bait and throws them over the side of the boat as well. The empty bait bags go into the bait barrels to be filled for the next set of traps. He threads the two freshly

20

baited bags into the emptied traps, snaps the lids closed, replaces the bungee cord, and lines the traps up to be dumped back overboard.

Meanwhile, Spencer has measured the carapaces, or shells, of the lobsters on his bulkhead. By law, to be sold in Maine, a lobster may measure no less than three and a quarter inches and no more than five inches from its eye sockets to the first joint on its back. From his years of experience, Spencer has a good eye and can judge many of the lobsters he hauls without measuring them with the brass gauge that Maine issues to all the state's lobstermen, but in every trap are lobsters so close to these limits that Spencer knows he cannot trust his eyes alone. Those that measure within the size limits are banded and tossed with the day's catch; those that fall short or long are returned to the sea.

While he works, Spencer divides his attention among the traps he is emptying, the position of his boat to the wind and tides and rocks, and the location of the next set of traps to be hauled. Never does his attention rest solely on the task at hand. By the time the last lobster from this first pair of traps is measured and the traps are fully emptied and rebaited, Spencer has spotted the buoy marking the second set of traps in this cluster, or string. Already he is throttling up and moving toward it. As the boat pulls away from the location of the traps just emptied, the traps are dumped one by one back over the rail. Less than a minute and a half has passed since Spencer gaffed the buoy for the first set of traps, and already he is on his way to the next set. The warp at his feet whistles as it follows the traps back toward the ocean floor.

And so it goes. Spencer and Bobby will haul, empty, sort, dump, and rebait each of the five to ten pairs of traps in this string and then move on to the next string. In summer, when the shallow water along the shore of the island is warm, the lobsters gather in the rocks here. Spencer and Bobby work their way now up and down the island's inlets and along its rough coast, weaving their way between boulders and other lobstermen's buoys. When he pauses to haul near land, Spencer always keeps the fragile bow, or front, of the boat headed away from the rocks, just in case the engine dies and the waves beat the boat toward shore.

By seven-fifteen, Spencer and Bobby have hauled their first hundred traps. The sun has risen over the far lip of water like a golden peach and is burning away the fog. The day brightens and so does Spencer's mood. He and Bobby celebrate by taking five minutes to eat breakfast. They rummage through the bag of food Wendy has packed for the day and find what they are looking for: Pepsi, crackers with peanut butter, and crabmeat sandwiches. Lunch, when it comes and if they stop to eat it, will be more of the same.

During this brief and rare break in the day's hauling, Spencer checks in at home on his citizens band radio. Before the invention of the CB radio, lobstering was lonely and isolating work. It is still solitary work, but the radio

22

fills a lobsterman's long hours with chatter. Even when Spencer is not using the radio himself, it squawks away, keeping him informed of the movements and activities of other lobstermen in the Swans Island fleet. Usually the conversations are light-hearted. Lobstering is a fiercely competitive but friendly business among lobstermen of the same fleet, and they joke with each other frequently throughout the day. However, the radio is also a lifeline in times of trouble, when engines fail or gas runs low or someone is hurt or lost overboard into the bone-chilling water. Spencer even recalls when the CB radio was his alarm clock. In the days when his mother and father lobstered together, the two of them would be off in the dark mornings long before Spencer and his sister had to rise to go to school. Then his mother would call in on the radio, asking, "Are you kids up yet?" While they stumbled from bed, she would give them the day's instructions.

Today Spencer learns from Wendy that Josh is long-gone to the wharf and is already out lobstering on his grandfather's boat, *The Prince of Peace*. Twelve-year-old Jaime and ten-year-old Emmie are finishing their morning chores, feeding and watering the dogs, chickens, and rabbits, before walking up the road to the post office to see what mail has come in on the morning ferry. Wendy is in the kitchen baking, as she does nearly every summer day, for her mother's small luncheonette.

Summer on Swans Island is idyllic. The days are long and warm, filled with the blinding blue of the sky and water. The air is constantly stirring, carrying the musty smell of fir forests, the salty scent of the ocean, and at low tide, the slightly sweet odor of seaweed stranded on the shores. Blueberry bushes line the roads, ripe for picking. Bald eagles soar high over Irish Point, taking in a sweeping view of islands that are scattered like confetti on the water. In quiet coves, where the rocks are warm and sun-drenched, seals heave themselves out of the brisk water and sprawl like sunbathers.

Day tourists who come over on the ferry on foot or bring their bikes to test their legs on some of the island's twenty-six miles of paved but hilly roads will be disappointed if they expect to find fast-food outlets, pizza parlors, or movie theaters. The island has none of these. Life here revolves around the school, the island's churches, and the wharf. Among the Joyce children, only Josh has ever been to a movie theater. That was nine years ago. However, tourists will discover that the island has its share of simple pleasures: Wendy's homemade blueberry pie at her mother's luncheonette, for example, or Spencer's stepmother's bed and breakfast, where they can watch the schooners sailing silently into the harbor in the summer's soft late-afternoon light.

The island has changed considerably since 1960, when the ferry began running regularly and attracting tourists to these remote shores, but the people of Swans Island have adapted to change before. Spencer's father, Llewellyn, is seventy-three. He remembers when he lobstered with wooden traps, wooden boats, and cork buoys before the days of wire traps, fiberglass boats, and Styrofoam buoys. He even remembers the days before lobstering was commercially practical. Sixty years ago, fish processing plants on Swans Island processed sixty thousand cod, mackerel, and sardines a day and shipped them off to ports along the coast and as far away as the Soviet Union. Like his father and grandfather before him and like the other fishermen of the island, Llewellyn was gone from home for days at a time then, trawling for fish along vast, invisible currents far out in the gulf. But the giant schools of mackerel eventually disappeared, and Swans Island fishermen were forced to find something new to harvest from the sea. They put away their huge nets and bought lobster traps. Now Llewellyn and the other lobstermen of the island chase lobsters and come home each night to their own beds.

To fill the long hours of hauling lobster traps, Josh's grandfather tells him stories of these earlier days. Josh knows that it once took a boatload of men rowing all day to pull a net the length of Toothacher Cove. When the boat reached the shore, horses were hitched to the corners of the net and coaxed to pull the heavily laden net onto the beach, where thousands of gasping scallops lay waiting to be harvested and sorted. He knows that a century ago Swans Island fishermen, his ancestors among them, each year took first or second place in the ranks of the Atlantic fishing fleet. This is Josh's history as well as the island's past, and he can recite it back six generations.

Josh is also learning a wealth of practical information from his father and grandfather. Since he started working beside them regularly four years ago, Josh has learned where to set his traps for the biggest catches and how to align a boat in relation to landmarks so as to know his position on the water. He has learned how to tie bowline knots and half hitches and when to use them, and how to read the sky and water for signs of trouble. Although Spencer says there are things about the sea that only time and experience

will teach Josh, he and Llewellyn are showing their faith in Josh's skill even now by teaching him to pilot their boats. In a business where a lobsterman's boat is as precious to him as his family, this is a compliment that speaks more loudly than words.

It is a hard day's work to stand all day lifting traps, streaming with water, over the side of the rail, but Josh doesn't see it that way. He has been on the water since he was a baby nestled in an empty lobster crate on his father's boat. The expanse of the sky, the mysteries of the ocean, and the vigor of the work are enough for Josh's imagination. He has to think hard to name something that he loves as much as lobstering.

From one of the traps set along a shoal well outside the harbor, Josh hauls an old female lobster. She is battered and bruised but berried, or seeded with thousands of lobster eggs, no larger than pinheads, that cling to her underside. She will carry these eggs for nine months, after which they will be released to develop into lobster larvae and eventually to mature into lobsters. Fewer than a half dozen eggs will survive to that point, and seven years will pass before any of them grows into a harvestable lobster. By law, Josh cannot keep her. Before he tosses her back, however, he uses his knife to cut a small notch in her tail. Any other Maine lobsterman who catches her in the future will know by the notch that she is a fertile lobster and must be returned to the ocean for breeding stock.

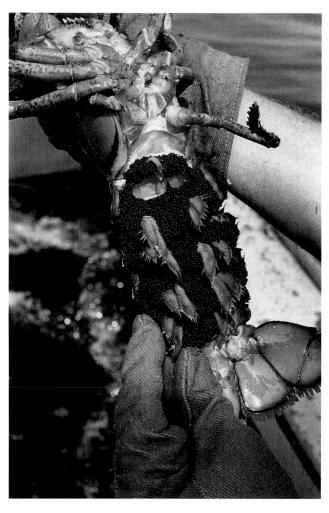

Later in the morning, Josh spots his father's boat near one of the offshore reefs. Like all lobster boats, it is surrounded by clouds of screaming seagulls who feast on the discarded bait. The two boats come up alongside each other so father, son, and grandson can swap opinions about the day's fortunes and conditions.

Llewellyn and Josh are pleased. They have hauled one hundred seventy traps since leaving the wharf at seven. Their day's hauling is nearly done, and they will be heading in soon to meet the lobstering truck, which Josh will help to load. Spencer and Bobby have hauled more than three hundred traps. Hours of work are left to empty all four hundred traps. With the slow start in the fog and the jobs still waiting to be done on the wharf, their work day

is stretching before them into the twilight like an endless and exhausting line. They decide to haul only a few more traps and then go meet the lobster truck. Tomorrow, Spencer will haul the traps he didn't reach today.

During the summer the lobster truck takes the ferry over from the mainland once or twice a week to collect the fleet's catch. Inside, the truck is refrigerated and moist because lobsters must be kept alive until they are cooked or they quickly develop poisons. Well into the last century lobstering was not practical on a large scale because no way existed to transport the lobsters live to the people in cities and towns down the coast and inland who wanted to eat them. These lobsters today will go to a lobster pound, a sealed-off cove along the coast, from which they will be sold to restaurants and stores.

Although the demand for fresh lobsters is high in the summer from all the tourists who come to the New England coast for vacations, the supply is limited. Summer, particularly late summer and early fall, is molting season for lobsters. Like all crustacea, and like the insects to which they are related, lobsters wear their skeletons on the outside. Each summer they grow another larger skeleton under the first one and shed their hard, old skeletons like pieces of outgrown clothing. The new shells are several sizes too large

for the muscles they contain, but by next summer the muscles will have grown too large for these skeletons, too, and the lobsters will be ready for another molt.

The shells at first are soft and thin as paper. The lobsters are easy prey now for crabs, sea urchins, and even other lobsters, who are not particular about what they scavenge from the ocean floor to eat. To protect themselves, they hide deep in the rocks on the ocean's bottom until their shells harden. Later in the fall, when most of the tourists have gone home and the demand for fresh lobsters has fallen off, the lobsters emerge from their hiding places in their newly hardened shells as bold and invincible as knights in armor. This is when lobstermen find them abundant, and the lobster truck will have to come to the island two and sometimes three times a week to carry away the fleet's catch.

In the early afternoon back at the wharf, Spencer and Bobby, Llewellyn and Josh weigh in their day's catch on the wharf's large scales. Newly molted soft-shelled lobsters bring a lower price per pound because their shells are only half filled with edible muscle, or meat. Hard-shelled lobsters, whose muscles fill a higher proportion of their shells, are worth more because they

contain more meat. Carefully, Spencer and Josh sort their lobsters into crates, which are loaded onto the truck.

By late in the afternoon, when most people would be willing to call the past twelve hours a day's work, Spencer goes to wash down his boat and load the next day's bait. Llewellyn does the same. Josh brings his skiff around, and he and Bobby head out to haul their own traps.

Like his father and grandfather before him, Josh has been hauling his own traps since he was old enough to pilot a skiff and pull the forty-pound traps off the ocean floor. In a jar under the skiff's seat is his lobstering license, and in his pocket is the brass measuring gauge that goes with it. He has the skiff his father had when he was a boy learning to lobster, and he has the twenty

37

lobster traps that his parents have given him for Christmas and birthday presents. He even has his own lobster buoy colors. Until this year, Josh used the same white and red combination that his great-grandfather used on his buoys. This year, however, Josh added lime green to the spindle on his buoys to help him distinguish them from those of another lobsterman in the Swans Island fleet.

Bobby has sixty traps of his own that he hauls by hand with Josh. Although Bobby has three times as many traps as Josh does, they split the profits from their afternoon's hauling half-and-half because Josh must pay the expenses for bait and fuel and for the care of his boat and engine. During the slower summer season, they haul their eighty traps every other day. In autumn, when the lobstering season is at its peak, they haul every day after Josh comes home from school and Bobby comes in from a day's hauling with Spencer. On any day, it is hard work to haul a heavy trap hand over hand through forty or fifty feet of water.

It is early evening before Josh and Bobby finish hauling their traps, sorting the lobsters, rebaiting, and dumping the traps again. Llewellyn sits on his porch overlooking the harbor, his own lobstering day finished, and waits for Josh to come in. The light softens, shadows lengthen, and warm breezes riffle across the harbor, puckering it with dimples. Finally, amid all the purring sounds of lobster-boat engines moving around in the harbor, Llewellyn catches the voice of Josh's skiff coming from around the head of a cove near the mouth of the harbor. Llewellyn's day is over now. He can go inside and eat. Josh is safely home.

When the first European settlers arrived on the coast of New England three hundred years ago, they found lobsters swarming over the tidal rocks. Some of the lobsters were five and six feet long, with crusher claws so powerful that nothing in the sea could hurt them. At low tide, the settlers gathered the smaller lobsters by hand. During high season, they ate them as commonly as crackers.

Today the lobstermen of Maine harvest twenty million pounds of lobsters each year, but the lobsters they catch are much smaller and more scarce. Lobsters are no longer the food of peasants but a luxury. The Joyces eat them no more than four or five times a year. Sometimes, lobsters are so scarce that few people eat them at all. Spencer and Wendy remember a season when the haul was so small that the family was short of money for groceries. That year, they ate whatever fish Spencer brought home from his traps at the end of the day.

Dinner at the Joyce's tonight is a steaming basketful of fresh clams and the day's catch, boiled to a bright red and served with lemon butter, topped off with some of Wendy's cookies that didn't make their way to the luncheonette. Josh and Bobby arrive just in time to bow their heads with the rest of the family. This is the time each day when the Joyces join hands and give thanks for the bounty of the sea that provides their living and for the grace that has brought them and their boats safely home. There is nothing idle about their prayers. The cemeteries of Swans Island are dotted with the headstones of men, some women, and even a few entire families who were lost at sea. The risks the Joyces take every day are great, and they are grateful for the evenings that find them seated once again around the table.

Talk is mostly swap and shop. Jaime isn't fond of lobster and bargains around the table to fill her plate with something else to eat. Emmie especially likes the lobster legs. Her father trades the thin legs of his lobster for the fat claws of hers, which like lobster tails are filled with meat that is slightly sweet and milky white. Everyone trades stories about the day's work and arranges

tomorrow's. They agree that Bobby will stay ashore to work on the house he is building on the island and that Josh will help him. Emmie and Jaime, who enjoyed the fine day today by swimming with their mother at one of the island's sandy beaches, will lobster with their father tomorrow to help him haul the traps he could not reach today.

Like Joshua, Jaime and Emmie have been on boats since they were babies. When they rise at dawn the next morning to go with their father to the wharf, they are retracing steps they have taken since they were seven or eight and old enough to bait bags. On board the boat, they find the gear that will keep them warm and dry, and they begin stuffing herring cuttings into their father's knitted bait bags even as the first light of day makes the morning fog shimmer and glow.

When Jaime and Emmie's father and grandfather were young, every boy on Swans Island had his own lobstering operation. Most graduated to become their fathers' sternmen and eventually bought big boats of their own and struck out alone. Daughters also learned to lobster from their fathers, and wives knew how to stand in as their husband's sternmen when labor was short. Before she died, Spencer's mother worked for years as Llewellyn's sternman, and in the years since, his stepmother has worked beside Llewellyn when she was needed. Wendy, whose family has been fishing on Swans Island even longer than Spencer's, grew up helping out on her father's lobster boat. When she married Spencer at the peak of the lobstering season, she understood without being told that he could spare only two days from tending

44

his traps for a honeymoon if they were to make it through their first winter together. In the years since, she has worked as Spencer's sternman when her help was needed.

Times have changed, however. The growing population on Swans Island has created jobs, such as carpentry and plumbing, that are not tied to the sea. Fewer boys now have the kind of small lobstering operation that Josh has or work beside their father as Josh does. Emmie and Jaime are two of only three girls on the island who lobster with their fathers, and it makes them feel special. They know they come from a long line of women — mother, grandmothers, aunts — who have proven the value of their work on the water.

Part of the lure is economic. Spencer has always paid his children for their work. The money the girls earn today will help pay for the overnight camp they will be attending on the mainland in a few weeks. But they are drawn to the water for other reasons, too. Like their father, they enjoy the freedom and beauty of being on the water with seagulls in the air and breezes blowing in from the ends of the earth.

Emmie feels, too, the pull of work that she enjoys. She doesn't mind digging her gloved hands into the barrel of herring cuttings and stuffing the broken fish into her father's orange bait bags. Everything about the island and her family's life on it, including lobstering, calls her back when she leaves. In a few years, when Josh graduates to a bigger boat, Emmie hopes to inherit his skiff and a few traps that she can call her own. She imagines herself grown and living on the island all her life, finding pleasure as her ancestors have for close to two centuries in the deep silences of its nights, the constant newness of its landscape, and the clockwork sighing of its tides.

Jaime has other dreams. Her nose is more sensitive to the rich smell of the bait and she is less willing to reach deep into a barrel of staring fish eyes,

46

but she knows her father needs her help today if he is to finish hauling the traps he wanted to reach yesterday. This is her part in her family's work, and she understands that. Still, she hopes one day to be a teacher. If she can find work at the island's school, she thinks that would be nice, but if she can't, she will look elsewhere. The island population has always risen and ebbed, like its tides, with the coming and going of people like Emmie and Jaime.

Even if she leaves the island, however, Jaime will carry away some of its special landscape in her memories. As they haul traps this morning, Spencer reports that they are over the Chimney Piece or the Graveyard Bottom or Grandpa's Shoals. There is nothing to see, of course, but the flat expanse of cold, gray water, but Spencer wants his children to know that the ocean floor lying beneath them is a rich and varied landscape of shoals and ledges, valleys and hidden mountain peaks. Over the centuries, the fishermen of Swans Island have given names to these invisible features. With many of the names comes a story. None of this is written down anywhere. Even fishermen from

the next island would know no more about the underwater landscape around Swans Island than what they could read on a nautical chart, but the names are part of the special life and lore of this small island, and Spencer passes it along like a gift to his children.

The fog lifts early, and the hauling goes quickly. Emmie and Jaime take turns baiting bags and emptying traps. Spencer is patient and gentle with his children. He wants them to understand and appreciate lobstering, so he gives them encouragement and time to learn. By noon, *The Daily Bread* is back at

the wharf, and Spencer is unloading some of the twenty thousand pounds of lobsters he will haul this year. It is clearly a day to do something special, and the Joyces will take advantage of the opportunity. They will go out for an early dinner.

Life on a small island is full of complications that people who live on the mainland would hardly be able to imagine. There is no island doctor or hospital, for example. Two doctors take turns visiting the island every other week to offer checkups, and the Swans Island ambulance, even in emergen-

cies, must ride the ferry like every other vehicle that makes the watery passage. The music teacher at the school takes the ferry on and off the island every Monday. Twice a month, Wendy goes to the mainland to run errands. Jaime goes to the mainland once a month to visit the orthodontist. It is most of a day's trip, since the appointment must be juggled with the ferry schedules.

Going out for dinner tonight means taking the lobster boat twenty minutes away to a neighboring island. Frenchboro's year-round population is less than a hundred, but unlike Swans Island, it has a small take-out restaurant at its wharf. The Joyces can tie up and walk up the dock to order crab cakes and ice cream and to visit with other lobstermen and their families.

Wendy and Spencer realize how important it is to get off the island occasionally. Each summer they take the family down the coast to North Haven, another island, for the annual lobster-boat races. They spend the day watching friends and neighbors compete, and then they sleep overnight on their boat. Each winter they spend a weekend or two at a motel on the mainland, shopping and eating out and washing off some of the island's deep winter isolation in the motel's heated indoor pool. Early each summer, before the lobstering season picks up, the family takes a car trip into New England. Sometimes they head north into Canada to other islands, Prince Edward and Grand Manan, where they have relatives to visit. Each of the trips shows the children that the world has horizons where water and sky do not always meet in a thin blue line.

Everything is different on Swans Island in autumn. The tourists and summer residents have gone home. They leave behind shuttered, empty houses with windows as dark and blank as new blackboards. The light is still bright, even blinding some days, but without the summer's warmth. Bright-yellow birch leaves drift across the quiet roads. School has reopened. Twice each day a school bus lumbers over the island's roads, through each of the three villages, picking up and discharging the island's fifty children, all of whom attend one central school.

Even the lobsters are on the move. When Spencer and Bobby head out now, they leave later in the morning and travel farther than they did in mid-summer when the days were long and warm. As the water in the shallows around the island has cooled, the lobsters have gone in search of warmth. They find it several miles from shore in water that is one hundred feet deep or more. Week by week through the autumn and into winter, Spencer and Bobby must move their traps farther and farther out to keep ahead of the migrating lobsters.

Ten miles out, with nothing on the eastern horizon but one hundred forty miles of water between his boat and the coast of Nova Scotia, Spencer finds it more difficult to use the visible land to get his bearings. He relies more

now on his compass and radar and the enormous map he carries around in his mind of this watery landscape. He claims to have been born with the chart in his head, but he knows its contours have been drawn and shaded in his memory over his years of trapping along the ocean's bottom. Even with all this, when he is fishing this far out, he sometimes has to rely on his loran C, a navigational instrument that provides precise degrees of latitude and longitude that help him find his way to these distant buoys even through fog and foul weather.

This is the peak of the lobstering season. Unlike the summer, when Spencer had to throw back three-quarters of the lobsters he caught because they were snappers, or undersize, he can keep half of what he catches now. Most lobsters have finished molting. Their shells are hard and firm with meat. The lobsters themselves feel bold in their new armor and readily leave the rocks where they have been hiding to feast on the lobstermen's bait. Each day Spencer returns to the wharf with barrels empty of herring and brimming with squirming lobsters. If the weather is fair, he will haul traps every day but Sunday and earn most of his year's income in the span of a dozen weeks.

Fishing farther out, Spencer sees less of the other thirty-four boats in the Swans Island fleet. They are all scattered in a wider circle around the island now, and the boats are often distinguishable in the distance only by the cloud of seagulls that keeps every lobsterman company. When two lobstermen pass close enough to each other to wave, they always do.

Like the other lobstermen in the fleet, Spencer waves with the fingers of his hand spread wide and his arm held stiff. It is a friendly wave of greeting, but it is something more, too. It says, "Hello! I'm fine. How are you?" The wave of the other lobsterman replies, "Hello! I'm fine. Thanks for asking." If the other lobsterman does not reply with a wave, Spencer will take off his

hat and wave more vigorously. So great are the dangers out here and so strong the feelings of loyalty and friendship within the island's fleet, that if the other lobsterman still does not reply, Spencer will pause in his hauling and bring his boat up alongside the other to make sure that everything is all right.

Every day now, the work of lobstering becomes harder. The days are shorter. The water is rougher. The traps are deeper, so the warps are longer. The weather is less predictable. By late October, the lobsters have moved too far out for Josh to chase in his skiff. It is time for him to pull his traps out for the season.

Last spring Josh completed his eighth and last year of school on the island and graduated to high school on nearby Mount Desert Island. This fall he has risen each morning in darkness and with five other Swans Island ninth-graders boarded the ferry for the ride to school. In the afternoon, he has returned on the ferry and hauled traps with Bobby into the twilight. In late October, he heads out to haul his traps for the last time this year. He and Bobby pull each trap from the bottom, empty it of any lobsters, and coil the warps inside. They pile the traps in the bow of the skiff and bring them back to the wharf to wait out the winter. Soon Josh will pull his skiff out as well and work only as his grandfather's sternman into the early days of winter.

At this time of year, both Joshua and Spencer unload their day's catch into a lobster car floating in the harbor. Cars are large submerged wooden pens anchored in the harbor where lobstermen store their lobsters until they can

get a favorable price for them. Since more people want fresh lobsters in the summer, when there are few lobsters to be caught, prices are high. In autumn, when lobsters are abundant, the tourists have gone home, and the smaller demand makes lobster prices drop. By storing their lobsters in a car and feeding them herring and brim, or redfish, each week, Spencer and Josh can keep their lobsters alive into early winter, when lobsters will again be scarce and difficult to catch. Then prices will rise once more.

Lobstering is full of risks, and the sea is only one of them. The unpredictability of lobster prices and the uncertainty of the size of the day's catch

are two others. Spencer can remember the day he hauled one hundred fifty traps and caught only three lobsters he could keep. But he also remembers another day when he hauled nine hundred eighty pounds of lobsters. And Llewellyn recalls when the price of lobster was as low as ten cents per pound. Yet Spencer still smiles when he talks about the time lobster reached six dollars per pound. Every day the Joyces juggle. Every day they hope for the best.

Each night, at the wharf or at home by telephone, Spencer checks the day's lobster prices. He and Josh discuss whether the price is likely to go up or down and whether they should sell the day's catch, empty out the whole car, or wait for a better price and hope it comes. When he has a thousand pounds of lobsters living in his car, a difference of only thirty cents per pound means the difference of several hundred dollars to Spencer. Although the quantity of lobsters Josh hauls is considerably less, he has his own books to keep, his own finances to manage, and his own expenses to pay, including

his school clothes to buy and monthly payments to make on a bank loan he took out to purchase a four-wheel all-terrain vehicle to ride in his free time. Among the many things Josh has learned from his father and grand-father is that a lobsterman must be as sensitive to the business of lob-stering as he is to the moods of the sky.

Now that daily lobstering is over for Josh for the season, his life is more like that of most teenagers, except that he will now move to Mount Desert Island to attend school for the winter. As the weather grows poorer and the days shorter, Josh can

no longer count on commuting each day to school on the ferry. Like most of his island classmates, he boards on Mount Desert through the winter months. He has been invited this year to live with one of the island's former teachers and her husband above his pharmacy in Southwest Harbor. Josh will continue to come home on weekends, but during the week for the next six months he will live, as he never has before, in a small village with real traffic, parking lots where he can ride his skateboard, and stores that he can walk to. His five hundred classmates at school will be from five islands, three of them smaller than Swans Island, and the fifth one, Mount Desert Island itself, large and close enough to be connected to the mainland by a bridge.

Although she loves the quiet and peacefulness of the island, Jaime is eager for the opportunity Josh has this year to discover a way of life that is, for all practical purposes, mainland living. The nine grades at the Swans Island school are grouped into three classrooms, and Jaime is now in the last of the three classes. The only other students in her grade are five girls. Emmie, in the middle class, has been the only girl in her grade since kindergarten, but she is not in any hurry to follow her brother off the island. Emmie enjoys the feelings of closeness in a community where she is related to three-quarters of her neighbors.

These years could change Josh's life, but he doesn't think they will. His family's veins are too full of salt water for him to imagine a life other than the one he's living. Skimming over the water in his skiff, he daydreams of when he will go to work full time for his father as sternman and of the day even

60

further away when he will have saved enough money and learned enough to buy his own big boat. Even now, he tells his island's history with his eye on the part he expects to play in it someday.

Winter settles over the island like a worn blanket that offers little warmth and less comfort. The days are short and often dark. Cold winds sweep down from the north and roil the seas into a lather of white froth and deep troughs. Sometimes the weather is too wild for the ferry to run. The coves and inland ponds freeze. Along the shore, the tides and relentless waves break the ice into large cakes that lie stranded on the rocks like abandoned automobiles. When winter is especially cruel, even Burnt Coat Harbor begins to freeze, first near the wharf and then gradually farther out, forcing the lobster boats to smash their way out from their moorings each morning.

All but a half dozen of the island's lobstermen pull their traps during the heart of winter and stack them on the wharf or in their front yards. Llewellyn no longer takes the risks that lobstering in winter involves. He spends the long, cold months of winter knitting bait bags — an art he learned from his father but one that few lobstermen practice anymore — or stringing the netting that traps the lobsters inside the metal traps. He repaints his lobster buoys, and if a mild day comes along, he works on his boat, readying it for the new season.

Spencer is too impatient to stack all his traps on the wharf and ride out the winter in a chair at home, but he is also too wise after three decades of lobstering to leave all his traps in. He knows he will be lucky if the weather allows him to haul once a week, and he also knows that in their constant search for warmth, the lobsters have migrated to water almost two hundred feet deep and fifteen miles out into the Gulf of Maine. So Spencer makes a compromise with the season. He moves out just the number of traps he can haul in a single good day to the deep water far from Swans Island, and then he hopes for fair enough weather to be able to reach them once a week. Now in the mornings he travels an hour or more to his traps before he can begin hauling and then works his way back toward the island, knowing that if bad weather suddenly overtakes him later in the day, he will be closer to port and safety. This is what his father taught him and what he is teaching Josh.

Lobstering in winter is nothing like lobstering in summer, when the sun is warm on Spencer's face and the waters are busy with the bobbing of other lobster boats. Now the weather can be so fierce the lobstermen call it poison. Spencer and Bobby will leave in darkness and return in darkness, guided by instinct, compass, and the mournful tolling of channel buoys that sing of

66

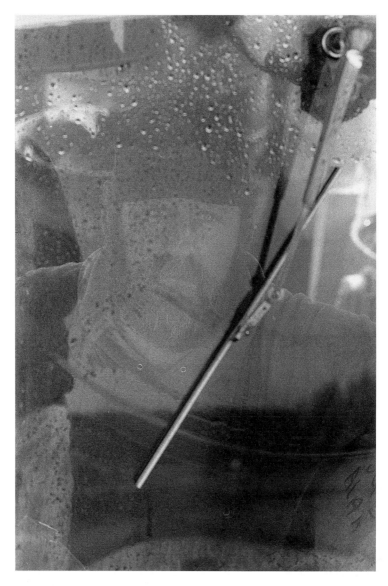

places where no boat should ever go. The warps are much longer than they were in summer and take much longer to haul, even with the help of the hydraulic hauler. Salt spray freezes on the thick beard Spencer has grown to protect his face. His hands, in and out of the cold water all day long, grow numb. To warm them, he plunges his gloves into the boat's steaming radiator water, wrings them out, and puts them back on his hands.

Even the water looks different in winter. In summer the water is blue from a distance except on cloudy days when it takes on the steely gray of the sky. Up close, however, it is the color of jade, clouded with the movement of millions of microscopic sea plants and animals. In winter the cloudiness clears. The green water is a flawless, transparent jewel through which the traps emerge from the dark depths like sunken treasure. But the water's beauty is deceiving. A lobsterman unfortunate enough to fall overboard, as some do every year, will freeze in five minutes if he doesn't drown first.

On days when he can't haul traps, Spencer paints buoys in his shed on the wharf or repairs traps. He also uses these days to work on his boat. And almost every day he delivers fuel oil to his neighbors on the island. Income from the oil deliveries helps tide the family over during the lean months of hauling.

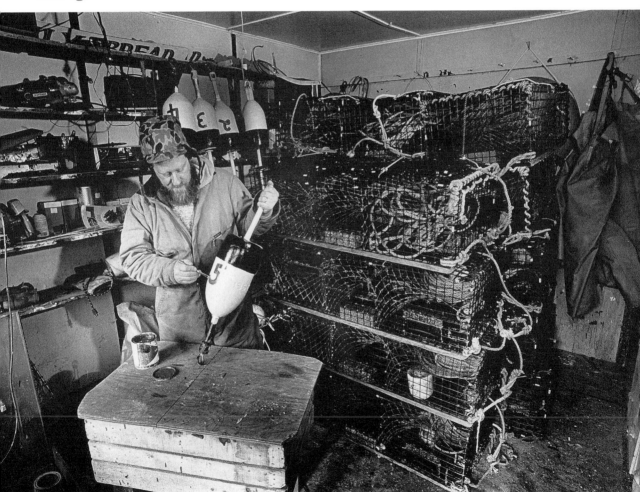

The winter days are quiet but not empty. Jaime continues her piano and guitar lessons. Emmie gathers with friends after school for quilting lessons at a neighbor's house. On weekends, Josh roams the winter-wasted fields, startling deer from his ATV. On Sunday afternoons, when the island's freshwater ponds are frozen as smooth and clear as sheets of glass, everyone laces up ice skates.

While Josh is home on weekends in January, the time comes to empty the lobster car in the harbor. All through the months of abundant lobsters in late fall, Spencer and Josh have been hoarding their autumn catch in the car. At the end of a good season, they may have forty-five hundred pounds of lobsters floating in the harbor's icy water. Now, when the supply of lobsters is low and the price begins to rise, Spencer and Josh know it is time to sell.

Bailing the cars is a family activity. The temperatures are often frigid, but the work is hard enough to keep everyone warm. Jaime and Emmie stack empty lobster crates on the rail of the boat as it floats beside the car in the harbor. Josh scoops the lobsters out of the car with a long dip net, and Wendy helps load them into the lobster crates. Spencer and Bobby lift the crates back aboard the boat and stack them for the short ride to the wharf, where they will be loaded onto larger boats or trucks and taken to a lobster pound.

The cycle of income in lobstering families is such that the money the Joyces receive for this large sale will have to carry them through to the start of summer when the lobsters once again become abundant enough to make hauling them profitable. With the income the Joyces receive for this sale, they will pay all their bills ahead to June. Even Josh will pay ahead on the bank loan he took out for his four-wheeler until he can start hauling again and earning money.

The cycle will be repeated in late spring. Although the lobsters are becoming more abundant in May and June and moving toward the warming water of the shore, the tourists have not yet come to the late-blooming Maine coast, and demand is still low. Through these months Spencer and Josh will once again hoard their lobsters in a car in the harbor until the tourist season starts in early July, causing demand, and prices, to soar. Then Spencer and Josh will sell off their spring catch, and the Joyces will once again pay their bills ahead until the season peaks in mid-autumn.

Sometime in late February the winds shift. Change blows in on the new, warmer currents. Deep in the rocks out in the gulf, the lobsters mysteriously sense the warmer air flowing over the water and begin to migrate back toward the shallow water around the island's shore. The old-squaw and other ducks who have come down from Labrador and the Arctic to winter off the coast of Maine take wing back home, to places where spring has yet to come and may never arrive. The coves and bays unlock. Low tide again exposes mud flats whose ripe smells are released to ride the spring breezes.

Everyone on the wharf is stirring. It is the start of a new lobstering season. Men who pulled their traps out two and three months ago when the lobsters moved to the rocks far offshore, now

75

head out again. The sterns of their boats are loaded with fantastic towers of freshly repaired traps and bouquets of brightly colored lobster buoys.

The Joyces also feel the currents of change that carry the island along in their grasp. Josh begins talking about moving home and putting his skiff back in the water. He is impatient to feel the throttle in his hand again and the skiff bouncing beneath him over the waves. Already he imagines the rocky ledges and protected gulleys his father and grandfather have shown him, special places where he will put his traps when the weather becomes fair enough for him to start lobstering after school again. Emmie wonders if she has grown enough this winter to be given a trap or two of her own to haul. Spencer trims his beard, as he does at the start of every lobstering season. He also takes the hundred traps that have been anchored far out in the gulf and the three hundred traps that have been sitting on the wharf through the winter and moves them to his favorite spring lobstering grounds. If the weather holds, he will begin hauling traps three and possibly four times a week.

But this spring the Joyces face more changes than usual. Bobby has had the unexpected opportunity to buy the boat and equipment of a part-time lobsterman on the island who is moving away. So Bobby will go out on his own. Sooner than he had expected, Josh is graduating to become his father's chief sternman. For the next three years, until he graduates from high school, Josh will lobster beside his father on weekends and during school vacations and haul his own traps in the short hours that remain. Wendy has volunteered to go along as Spencer's sternman during the week if she is needed. Jaime and Emmie know their help will be needed more often, too. Llewellyn will take on Josh's cousin, Justin, as his sternman.

All three generations of the Joyces will do whatever is necessary to stay on Swans Island and continue lobstering. This has been their family's home for close to two hundred years, and they cannot imagine any other. Neither can they imagine any other way of life. Early each spring, when the frigid waters begin stirring again with life, it has always been time for the Joyces to go down to the sea in their boats. Regardless of the ever-changing dance of light, the eternal play of the wind, and the everlasting rhythm of the tides, the sea has always provided a living for those brave and strong enough to claim it. This much doesn't change.

Acknowledgments

Many people helped to make this book possible, and we would like to thank them: Harriet, George, and Nathan Price, for countless arrangements and for pointing us toward the Joyces in the first place; Dale Kuhnert, for research; Peg Bailey, for sharing her knowledge of Swans Island; Helen Sanborn and the Swans Island School, for taking time with us; Maria Muller, for printing the photographs; the Newport Public Library of Newport, New Hampshire, for meeting space; the students of Charlotte Stocek's class at the Union Elementary School in Montpelier, Vermont, for their interest in and comments on the manuscript; Charlotte MacLeay and Helen and Don Benedict, for reading the manuscript; and the residents of Swans Island, who were unfailingly patient, friendly, and hospitable. We would like to thank particularly Jeannie and Llewellyn Joyce, who gave us breakfast at four o'clock in the morning and beds at the end of the day. Also, we would like to express our warm appreciation to all the Joyces — Spencer, Wendy, Joshua, Jaime, Emmie, Llewellyn, and Jeannie — and to Wendy's mother, father, and brother, all of whom took us in as if we were family. We are deeply grateful.